T0025965

# ABUSE OF LANGUAGE,
# ABUSE OF POWER

JOSEF PIEPER

# ABUSE OF LANGUAGE
# ABUSE OF POWER

Translated by
Lothar Krauth

IGNATIUS PRESS   SAN FRANCISCO

Title of the German original:
*Mißbrauch der Sprache*
*Mißbrauch der Macht*
First edition © 1974, Kösel-Verlag, Munich
This edition © 1988 by Schwabenverlag AG,
Ostfildern bei Stuttgart

Cover design by Roxanne Mei Lum
Cover border by Pamela Kennedy
Calligraphy by Victoria Hoke Lane

© 1992 Ignatius Press, San Francisco
ISBN 978–0–89870–362–7
Library of Congress catalogue card number 90–85240
Printed in the United States of America

# CONTENTS

# ABUSE OF LANGUAGE,
# ABUSE OF POWER

THE TOPIC OF THIS ESSAY can also be stated as "the abuse of language in its relation to the abuse of power". I intend to approach this subject from two different directions: though these are two distinct considerations, I shall nonetheless try to show their intrinsic connection.

One of these considerations is a phenomenon of classic antiquity, Plato's lifelong battle with the sophists, those highly paid and popularly applauded experts in the art of twisting words, who were able to sweet-talk something bad into something good and to turn white into black. They are those people whom Plato, in his *Dialogues,* puts in confrontation with Socrates. To be sure, historicity (don't worry!) is not my concern in this. It is rather Plato's position—and this indeed is the other consideration—which shall be taken as a paradigm showing, I believe, something directly relevant for us and our own situation today. The case can be made that Plato recognized, identified, and battled in the sophistry of his time a danger and a threat besetting the pursuits of the human mind and the life of society in any era.

Anything in what follows that may at first appear to be perhaps a mere historical description and interpretation should, therefore, in point of fact be taken as a commentary on the present. And further, then, anything that may at first sound like a mere critique of the present, aimed at our own situation, should also be taken as pointing to a timeless temptation that since the beginning of history has always required mankind's resistance and will require it forever. This timeless character of the sophistic phenomenon, transcending any particular age, prompted certain important, indeed disturbing, comments by Hegel. True, he called the sophists of Socrates' time "extremely refined and learned people"; but such praise, in Hegel's manner of speaking, sounds somewhat ambiguous. It is precisely such learned refinement, says Hegel, such absolute and unmoored questioning that plucks apart any object and dialectically discredits everything; it is such "refined reasoning" (*gebildetes Raisonnement*) — an expression repeatedly used by Hegel — that poses the true danger. It almost inevitably leads us, says Hegel, to the conviction that everything can be justified if we look hard enough for reasons. To quote Hegel: "You need not have advanced very far in your learning in order to find good reasons even for the most evil of things. All the evil deeds in this world since Adam and Eve have been justified with good reasons." Hegel, therefore, sees here a danger clearly intrinsic to the human mind, being part of its nature, a danger that can perhaps be overcome but never entirely avoided. And this danger could become all the more threatening, the more highly man's power of judgment, that is, his mental formation, is perfected. Granted, what the accepted monographs say about the sophists may indeed be correct: Werner Jäger, for one, sees in the sophists "the earliest humanists"; they have been praised as great educators and teachers, as the first advocates for the freedom of thought, and so on. All this may well be entirely correct. And yet, it is precisely here where the danger lurks: only within the framework of those achievements can this specific destruction be wrought, a destruction that Hegel, too, has in mind when using the term *sophistry*. In this, the German philosopher is clearly siding with Plato. Both discuss something relevant beyond a specific era; both identify a danger threatening the human mind and commonweal at any time.

But, of course, it is not only the sophist phenomenon itself that thus may assume an updated and contemporary interest and relevance; and as the human mind progresses in terms of ever greater "sophistication", so also will the sophist phenomenon probably become ever more acute.

"The sophists are not as remote to us as we may imagine", says Hegel. I wish to make this statement the implicit motto of my reflections here, this—and Nietzsche's posthumous line, "The era of the sophists? Our time!" To repeat, then: it is not only the sophistic mentality itself that in this context arouses renewed interest but also, and even more so, Plato's argumentation, his contention with the sophists. Why, indeed, was he so dead set against the sophists? In what did he see their evil influence? What exactly did he feel they threatened? What is it, in Plato's opinion, that must never be sacrificed, under any circumstances, if man is to lead a truly human existence? Again: What did Plato have against the sophists?

The outward appearance of these men, as depicted in Plato's *Dialogues,* is sufficiently known. But there are rather obvious traits and others not so obvious, and some may only seem to be obvious.

To begin with, we notice the fact that these men are exceptionally successful, which every now and then prompts the sardonic admiration on the part of Socrates. He notices this merchandising of wisdom, this disregard of the essential difference between money and the spirit, as if there were no difference between what used to be called *artes liberales,* the liberal arts, and what we now call "mental work"; as if there were no difference between honorarium and wages. This consideration is much more relevant than may appear at first. Bertrand Russell, in his *History of Western Philosophy,* observes rather contemptuously that those professors should get down from their high horse when they denounce the sophists because they accepted payments; the professors themselves take money, he says, and quite a lot of it. But this still does not capture the crucial point. The crucial point, the incommensurability, is not mentioned here. A casual remark by Socrates is much more on target. The Cratylus dialogue, which incidentally also discusses the problem of language, deals with a certain question that for us here is of no consequence, and Socrates remains silent. Finally they ask him, "And what do you think, Socrates?" To which he replies, "I have no opinion on this, for I could afford only the five-drachma lecture of Prodicus [one of those great sophists!]. His fifty-drachma lecture I could not afford; had I been able to, then perchance I might be knowledgeable." Here the crucial point is made loud and clear.

A few years ago, one of Einstein's friends published some recollections in the *Frankfurter Allgemeine,* in which he relates, among other things, what Einstein had once told him: "An American university has offered me half a million dollars for the twelve original handwritten pages of my theory of relativity. This offer really bothers me. How can one sell the achievements of the mind!" And Sartre, in the *Présentation* to the 1945 first issue of his magazine *Les Temps Modernes,* discusses the situation of the modern writer, indeed touching on many aspects but also on our specific subject. He says, "Why in the world are we ashamed, why do we blush, when money is mentioned? We simply receive our wages, as any other worker does!" Well, yes, a sonnet consists of fourteen lines. Will you be paid by the line, or by the hour, or by what standard? Maybe you needed only five minutes for it, maybe six months! The crucial point here is that money and mind are incommensurable. This has to be kept in mind, it seems to me, if this subject matter is to be discussed from Plato's standpoint.

Then there is this other aspect in the manner the sophists are presented: Plato depicts them, without exception, as strangely "handsome", these adversaries of Socrates, who himself is ugly like Silenus. But this beauty, mentioned with an irony quite untypical for classical Greece, seems to point to something much more fundamental, much less obvious as well. The dialogue *Protagoras* begins with Socrates' telling about the time when he returned from a party and met a friend who addressed him, "You look so excited, just as if you were coming from your handsome young friend Alcibiades." To which he replied, "Indeed, I am coming from a party where Alcibiades was also present. But I hardly paid attention to him; I did not even cast an eye on him. For, you see, there was someone so much more handsome, Protagoras"—the old sophist. This, of course, is meant as pure irony. Why should a classical Greek speak of physical beauty in an ironical tone? But worse is to come: ugliness receives praise—as resembling Socrates. There is this dialogue *Theaetetus*, a late writing. Together with a "visiting professor" who lectures on mathematics in Athens, Socrates is standing in front of a stadium in which a group of young men are getting dressed. And Socrates asks this Theodorus, "Did you notice among your listeners and students someone who is especially talented?" To which the other replies, "Yes, just one, but he is not, as you might think, the most handsome. On the contrary—he is quite ugly. He resembles you—the same flat nose, the same protruding eyes!" Then the lads come rushing out, and the one in question is called over by Theodorus. "Theaetetus," the name providing the title for the entire dialogue, "Theaetetus, do come here; Socrates desires to speak to you." And so this dialogue begins, progressing toward deep abstraction and speculation and becoming ever more difficult, until finally Socrates asks Theaetetus, "Now, please, show me what face *I* have. For Theodorus claims your face is similar to mine." This is arranged in such a roundabout manner as to warrant the question: What is Plato's purpose in all this? True beauty, of course, is not the subject of this irony here. It seems to me that we should understand this passage in a way similar to our notion of "perfection". Taken literally, "perfection" means "completion", "wholeness". But when we speak of "perfectionism", we really mean something negative, annoying, even dangerous. And the question as to what makes such perfectionism dangerous, applied to our topic, becomes the question: What indeed did Plato have against the sophists?

His objection could tentatively be summed up in these brief terms: corruption of the word—you are corrupting the language! Still, the core of the matter is not yet identified with this. The specific threat, for Plato, comes from the sophists' way of cultivating the word with exceptional awareness of linguistic nuances and utmost formal intelligence, from their way of pushing and perfecting the employment of verbal constructions to crafty limits, thereby—and precisely in this—corrupting the meaning and the dignity of the very same words.

Word and language, in essence, do not constitute a specific or specialized area; they are not a particular discipline or field. No, word and language form the medium that sustains the common existence of the human spirit as such. The reality of the word in eminent ways makes existential interaction happen. And so, if the word becomes corrupted, human existence itself will not remain unaffected and untainted.

What, however, does "corrupting the word" mean? This question can obviously be answered only after what constitutes the dignity and "import" of the word within the totality of human existence has been clarified.

Human words and language accomplish a twofold purpose, as Plato without doubt would have answered—in clear agreement with the entire tradition of Western thought. Since this accomplishment is twofold, we may already here suspect that the word's degeneration and corruption can also be twofold. First, words convey reality. We speak in order to name and identify something that is real, to identify it for *someone,* of course—and this points to the second aspect in question, the interpersonal character of human speech.

These two aspects of the word and of all language, though distinct, are nevertheless not separated. The one does not exist without the other. At first we may well presume that such and such is simply a factual reality and that all we want is to understand this reality and, of course, describe it. Right: describe it—but to whom? The other person is already in the picture; what happens here is already communication. In the very attempt to know reality, there already is present the aim of communication. And again, we may well presume at first that we are relating only to this one person we are addressing at one time. Still, what do we talk *about?* Indeed, we can talk only about reality, nothing else. Of course, there is also the possibility of lying, of falsifying! It is one of my favorite questions in tests, posed many times and not always answered to my satisfaction: Can a lie be taken as communication? I tend to deny it. A lie is the opposite of communication. It means specifically to withhold the other's share and portion of reality, to prevent his participation in reality. And so: corruption of the relationship to reality, and corruption of communication—these evidently are the two possible forms in which the corruption of the word manifests itself. Because of these two corruptions, precisely because of them, Socrates over and again chides the sophists' rhetoric, that artistry with words. This is, in Plato's dialogues, the constantly repeated lament and accusation (and to realize their astonishingly modern relevance, all we have to do is sum them up): reality, you think, should be of interest to you only insofar as you can impressively talk about it! And because you are not interested in reality, you are unable to converse. You can give fine speeches, but you simply cannot join in a conversation; you are incapable of dialogue!

Here, again, the one cannot be separated from the other. Any discourse detached from the norms of reality is at the same time mere monologue. What does it mean, after all, to be detached from the norms of reality? It means indifference regarding the truth. To be true means, indeed, to be determined in speech and thought by what is real. And I do not think it to be simply a suggestive literary touch—though Plato would not be above that—when in his dialogues he depicts the man who claims as his business the dealing with words, the formal cultivation of how best to employ words, as a nihilist: Gorgias! He is, of course, a historical figure. We do know some of the opening sentences of his writings, and the very first sentence states that "nothing is". This Gorgias does not by any means intend to deny the existence of countless facts that lead to even more countless news reports and commentaries. What he does intend to say is this: there is no such thing as *being,* endowed as it were with normative authority that the one who speaks would have to respect or would be able to respect!

The orientation toward reality, truth itself—and this is what it amounts to—can in all honesty not be the decisive concern of those who aim at verbal artistry. To raise such a question already reveals total ignorance of the essential requirements in the art of composing words.

"A writer can be defined as someone whose second nature is the conviction that the *content* of his thoughts and writings does not matter in the least." This statement—a very dogmatic statement, is it not?—is a quotation; it does not come from a sophist of Plato's dialogues but rather from an important contemporary German author. Gorgias could have said the same thing, as he in fact expressed a similar idea: What is decisive is not *what* you say but *how* you say it—its composition, its expression, its form. On the surface he is right, of course. It is not the subject matter but the creative form that constitutes the linguistic piece of art. Still, Plato's concern points toward something else, and he insists on it, and he challenges us with it, even challenging himself and his own profound sensitivity for linguistic form: the possibility that something could well be superbly crafted—that it could be perfectly worded; brilliantly formulated; strikingly written, performed, staged, or put on screen—and at the same time, in its entire thrust and essence, be false; and not only false, but outright bad, inferior, contemptible, shameful, destructive, wretched—and still marvelously put together!

Plato does not say, "If something is marvelously put together, then you should have your suspicions right away." No, he simply asks to be aware of the possibility of something's being superbly crafted and nevertheless sham and foul—unless, to quote Plato's Socrates, we define the linguistic artist as a speaker of truth. The very moment such a notion is spelled out, we are part of a controversy. *Controversy* would even be a very mild term for the ensuing reaction, not different from Plato's times.

Still, Socrates does not really trust the words of his conversation partner, Gorgias; he does not believe that verbal expressions, unconcerned about any truth, aim at nothing but pure form, daring images, superb style, and the achievement of new means of expression. The illusion, however, that this is the case, that exclusively or at least primarily this really happens—such a deceptive illusion may well persist for some time, within the ivory tower of a modern literary business, maybe even for an extended span of time. But Socrates compels Gorgias himself to debunk this pretense. He forces Gorgias to admit that such sophisticated language, disconnected from the roots of truth, in fact pursues some ulterior motives, that it invariably turns into an instrument of power, something it has been, by its very nature, right from the start.

And with this we have identified the other aspect of the corruption of the word: the destruction of its nature as communication. This particular issue, however, is somewhat obscured by the rather stilted terminology we have to put up with in all translations of Plato, especially in this particular area, so that the authentic message of Plato's reflections is grasped only with difficulty. There we read of the "art of persuasion", of "flattery", of "flattering speech" and the "art of flattery". Such talk, obviously, does not raise the proverbial eyebrows of anybody. (It was Hegel who declared that the task of philosophy is not at all to raise anybody's eyebrows, but my point here is to show the underlying, rather provocative, modern relevance.)

The very moment, as I have stated, that someone in full awareness employs words yet explicitly disregards reality, he in fact ceases to communicate anything to the other. This the reader may more or less have accepted. But an *instrument of power?* Is this not too strong and too overbearing an expression? It really implies that from one moment to the next the human relationship between the speaker and the listener changes. I have to say, yes, indeed, this is precisely what happens; this really is going on! Whoever speaks to another person—not simply, we presume, in spontaneous conversation but using well-considered words, and whoever in so doing is explicitly not committed to the truth—whoever, in other words, is in this guided by something other than the truth—such a person, from that moment on, no longer considers the other as partner, as equal. In fact, he no longer respects the other as a human person. From that moment on, to be precise, all conversation ceases; all dialogue and all communication come to an end. But what, then, is taking place? This very question is answered by Socrates with an old-fashioned term: *flattery*—what takes place could perchance be flattery! Now—"doggone", to stay with the Socratic idiom: What does that *flattery* mean? We no longer use this term in such a context; it has lost its bite, yet the subject matter itself is as relevant as ever.

What, then, is flattery? Flattery here does not mean saying what the other likes to hear, telling him something nice, something to tickle his vanity. And what is thus said is not necessarily a lie, either. For example, I might meet a colleague and say to him, "I have read your recent article, and I am fascinated!" It could well be that I have not read the article at all and am therefore anything but fascinated. This does not yet amount to flattery! Or else I might indeed have read the article, and I am really fascinated, and what I said *was* flattery nevertheless. In what lies the distinction? What makes the difference? The decisive element is this: having an ulterior motive. I address the other not simply to please him or to tell him something that is true. Rather, what I say to him is designed to *get* something from him! This underlying design makes the message a flattery, even in the popular meaning of the word. The other, whom I try to influence with what he likes to hear, ceases to be my partner; he is no longer a fellow subject. Rather, he has become for me an object to be manipulated, possibly to be dominated, to be handled and controlled. Thus the situation is just about the opposite of what it appears to be. It appears, especially to the one so flattered, as if a special respect would be paid, while in fact this is precisely *not* the case. His dignity is ignored; I concentrate on his weaknesses and on those areas that may appeal to him—all in order to manipulate him, to use him for *my* purposes. And insofar as words are employed, they cease to communicate anything. Basically, what happens here is speech without a partner (since there is no true other); such speech, in contradiction to the nature of language, intends not to communicate but to manipulate. The word is perverted and debased to become a catalyst, a drug, as it were, and is as such administered. *Instrument of power* may still seem a somewhat strong term for this; still, it does not seem so farfetched any longer.

The relevance of all this becomes evident as soon as we ask ourselves in what areas we might find such flattery nowadays. Immediately this counterquestion arises: Is there still *any* area of life at all free of it, any corner where I am spared such flattery designed to manipulate me—to make me buy something, for instance? And yet, the slogans of our advertisements may still be relatively harmless examples—maybe! Maybe it is after all not so harmless that this form of "communication" has become commonplace and is accorded a common place in our daily life. All the more questionable may be the fact that an "inside" knowledge, the psychoanalytical knowledge of man, is unscrupulously employed in this business. We should also consider how these ubiquitous commercials in turn possess the power to influence human attitudes, as these commercials propagate a dream-world primarily by glorifying human weaknesses. Not that we should see the devil in every corner. We may indeed deny any serious threat in a kind of flattery that emphasizes our obvious sophistication, acknowledges us as connoisseurs, as being "with it" and youthful and whatever else, just so we buy this brand of cigarettes, or that aftershave, or this specific whiskey. Still, it can hardly be denied that our language through all this indeed progressively loses its character as communication, as it more and more tries to influence while less and less saying anything. I have only to walk through any town or city and observe the billboards advertising cigarettes. All those slogans ("You've come a long way, baby!" "Smooth character!" "Come to where the flavor is!" "Alive with pleasure!") have nothing at all to do with the advertised product as such. They are simply nonsensical, yet they are no simple nonsense but rather an extremely calculated and highly financed nonsense! What should make us stop and think is the ease with which we buy all this—buy it in both meanings of the word.

The most genuine territory of sophistic flattery, however, is marked by a somewhat different approach, and concise terms to define it are difficult to find. Let me propose to analyze the concept of "entertainment" from just such a perspective. With this concept I do not mean here the fun and games designed for having a good time together. I do not mean at all something that is actively done and arranged but rather an area that is meant by the refreshingly frank though somewhat crude expression *entertainment industry*. I am talking about those special "consumer goods" marketed by a peculiar production apparatus that has made flattery its big business. We should not think only of the trivialities found in certain "popular" magazines and hit shows. On the contrary, "sophistic" implies a claim to the highest standards of form and refinement. But the matter, we have to admit, is all in all rather complicated. They not only "tickle your fancy" here, as everywhere else, to induce you to buy their product but also offer the flattery itself for sale and consumption. You are expected to pay for being flattered! And even this statement expresses the matter much too simply. The product for which I am ready to pay the price consists, strictly speaking, not only of the flattery that extols my own foibles. This, of course, is expected, but it should happen in such a manner that I remain unaware of what in truth is going on here. Of course, this is by definition one aspect of flattery; a flattery unmasked is all but a contradiction in terms. "The world wants to be deceived", the saying goes; *mundus vult decipi*. This is indeed true, yet at the same time too narrow. What the world really wants is flattery, and it does not matter how much of it is a lie; but the world at the same time also wants the right to disguise, so that the fact of being lied to can easily be ignored. As I enjoy being affirmed in my whims and praised for my foibles, I also expect credibility to make it easy for me to believe, in good conscience or at least without a bad conscience, that everything I hear, read, absorb, and watch is indeed true, important, worthwhile, and authentic!

Such, then, is the demand. To such a demand the supply has to respond if there is going to be a profitable business. Still, the demand is not concentrated only on what is commonly considered pleasing. There are not only sex, sensuality, vanity, nosiness, and sentimentalism; there are also cruelty and indeed *Schadenfreude,* the vicious enjoyment of others' misfortune. There are the obsession with slander, the frenzy to destroy, and the readiness to accept radical answers, to go for the "final solution". All these weaknesses need flattery. Yet not just any plain flattery, no—there has to be credibility; there have to be "convincing reasons", in Hegel's words. To succeed in such a task is without doubt a demanding enterprise. Even Socrates loses all his irony in conceding this point to the sophists: "You are truly experts in this; you must have a deep understanding of human nature; you know exactly which spot to hit."

Such an endeavor, however, clearly carries with it the promise of boundless success. It can obviously thrive only within the medium of language —language taken in its most general meaning: speech, song, print, pictures, movies, and broadcast. The entire arsenal of the means of communication can potentially be employed. All these established, even institutionalized possibilities to process communication are by their very nature designed to function as vehicles of genuine human speech; they are designed, therefore, to capture and communicate reality. I believe it would be entirely unjust to contend that this fundamental character of the word as a rule is betrayed and corrupted. Still, it is quite evident that the danger of corruption increases as the promise of possible success becomes more tempting. Not just a specific sector is then endangered, such as the press, or television, or radio; no, the commonweal of all people is then threatened, since by necessity it functions through the medium of the word. Then we are faced, in short, with the threat that communication as such decays, that public discourse becomes detached from the notions of truth and reality.

I said this danger is evident. It would be more correct, however, to say it is evident that there can be such a threat; unfortunately, the threat itself is not so readily recognized, for it is part of its nature to be concealed and disguised. It is, therefore, extremely difficult, at times impossible, to take a specific item (such as a novel, a stage play, a movie, a radio commentary, or a critical essay) and identify the borderline that separates genuine communication rooted in reality from the mere manipulation of words aimed solely to impress. Formal excellence alone cannot be the decisive criterion. A philosophical discourse, or notably even a theological discourse, can equally be listed here, especially when it draws its power from the element of surprise, when thus it exploits the general intellectual ennui. Yes, even philosophy, theology, and the humanities, just like any fictional literature, however demanding and challenging, in essence may well be mere entertainment in our specific sense here—that is, a form of flattery, extremely refined perhaps, yet nevertheless courting favor to win success. And success in this does not necessarily mean huge sales and large profits. Any form of approval will do, either the applause of the masses or the admiration of the "happy few".

Plato stated it repeatedly: the difficulty in recognizing a sophist at all is part of his success. So writes John Wild, the American scholar and expert on Plato: "The Sophist appears as a true philosopher, more so than the philosopher himself". How, then, can anyone be expected to tell which is which! Plato himself complicated this confusing picture even more, from the other end, as it were: "Is it not obvious", he wonders in his dialogue *Phaedrus,* "that even those who have a genuine message of truth and reality must first court the favor of the people so they will listen at all? Is there not such a thing as seduction to the truth?" Karl Jaspers, toward the end of his life, expressed his fear that one day it may become inevitable to dress truth itself in propaganda just so it will reach people's ears. And then there is Søren Kierkegaard, who, to be sure, should find us on guard, for he loved irony. In his late years he wrote a small volume, *On the Approach Employed in My Literary Activity,* in which he summed up this approach with: "Cajole them into the truth!" First, so says Kierkegaard, you have to tell them something nice, aesthetic, to capture people's attention—launch the boat, as it were. Then, when it is floating along, let it run aground: namely, on the rock of truth. Better hurry, though, to get away from there immediately; they will try to kill you.

Be this as it may—this much remains true: wherever the main purpose of speech is flattery, there the word becomes corrupted, and necessarily so. And instead of genuine communication, there will exist something for which *domination* is too benign a term; more appropriately we should speak of tyranny, of despotism. On one side there will be a sham authority, unsupported by any intellectual superiority, and on the other a state of dependency, which again is too benign a term. *Bondage* would be more correct. Yes, indeed: there are on the one side a pseudoauthority, not legitimized by any form of superiority, and on the other a state of mental bondage.

Plato evidently knew what he was talking about when he declared the sophists' accomplished art of flattery to be the deceptive mirage of the political process, that is, the counterfeit usurpation of power, a power that belongs to the legitimate political authority alone.

Of course, this cannot as yet be called use of force and exercise of power in a strict sense; it is not yet for real, as it were. But much less, at any rate, are we moving perchance within a neutral territory, separated from the political reality and labeled, say, "the press", or "the cultural domain", or "the field of literature", or whatever name one chooses. Public discourse, the moment it becomes basically neutralized with regard to a strict standard of truth, stands by its nature ready to serve as an instrument in the hands of any ruler to pursue all kinds of power schemes. Public discourse itself, separated from the standard of truth, creates on its part, the more it prevails, an atmosphere of epidemic proneness and vulnerability to the reign of the tyrant.

Serving the tyranny, the corruption and abuse of language becomes better known as *propaganda.* Here, once again though briefly, I have to mention Plato and the translation of Plato. Most translations have "the art of persuasion" in this context. Plato himself, however (in the *Politeia,* the great dialogue on the social and political order), characterizes the essence of injustice as the combination and collaboration of *peithō* and *bia,* rendered as "persuasive word" and "brute force". Obviously, something is lost when the translations speak only of cajoling, wheedling, and flattery. Left out is the element of menace. But then again, the most perfect propaganda achieves just this: that the menace is not apparent but well concealed. Still, it must remain visible; it must remain recognizable. At the same time, those for whom the menace is intended must nevertheless be led and eased into believing (and that is the true art!) that by acquiescing to the intimidation, they really do the reasonable thing, perhaps even what they would have wanted to do anyway.

All this is not outside our own experience. Yet propaganda in this sense by no means flows only from the official power structure of a dictatorship. It can be found wherever a powerful organization, an ideological clique, a special interest, or a pressure group uses the word as their "weapon". And a threat, of course, can mean many things besides political persecution, especially all the forms and levels of defamation, or public ridicule, or reducing someone to a nonperson—all of which are accomplished by means of the word, even the word not spoken. Karl Jaspers counted among the forms of "modern sophistry", as he calls it, also the "lingo of the revolution", which, "intent on fomenting rebellion through agitation, singles out one isolated instance, and focusing its spotlight on this, makes everyone blind to all the rest".

The common element in all of this is the degeneration of language into an instrument of rape. It *does* contain violence, albeit in latent form. And precisely this is one of the lessons recognized by Plato through his own experience with the sophists of his time, a lesson he sets before us as well. This lesson, in a nutshell, says: the abuse of political power is fundamentally connected with the sophistic abuse of the word, indeed, finds in it the fertile soil in which to hide and grow and get ready, so much so that the latent potential of the totalitarian poison can be ascertained, as it were, by observing the symptom of the public abuse of language. The degradation, too, of man through man, alarmingly evident in the acts of physical violence committed by all tyrannies (concentration camps, torture), has its beginning, certainly much less alarmingly, at that almost imperceptible moment when the word loses its dignity. The dignity of the word, to be sure, consists in this: through the word is accomplished what no other means can accomplish, namely, communication based on reality. Once again it becomes evident that both areas, as has to be expected, are connected: the relationship based on mere power, and thus the most miserable decay of human interaction, stands in direct proportion to the most devastating breakdown in orientation toward reality.

I spoke of public discourse becoming "detached from the notions of truth and reality". This brief characterization may still be too mild; it does not yet express the full measure of devastation breeding within the sophistic corruption of the word. It is entirely possible that the true and authentic reality is being drowned out by the countless superficial information bits noisily and breathlessly presented in propaganda fashion. Consequently, one may be entirely knowledgeable about a thousand details and nevertheless, because of ignorance regarding the core of the matter, remain without basic insight. This is a phenomenon in itself already quite astonishing and disturbing. Arnold Gehlen labeled it "a fundamental ignorance, created by technology and nourished by information". But, I wanted to say, something far more discouraging is readily conceivable as well: the place of authentic reality is taken over by a fictitious reality; my perception is indeed still directed toward an object, but now it is a *pseudoreality,* deceptively appearing as being real, so much so that it becomes almost impossible any more to discern the truth.

Plato's literary activity extended over fifty years, and time and again he asked himself anew: What is it that makes the sophists so dangerous? Toward the end he wrote one more dialogue, the *Sophist,* in which he added a new element to his answer: "The sophists", he says, "fabricate a fictitious reality." That the existential realm of man could be taken over by pseudorealities whose fictitious nature threatens to become indiscernible is truly a depressing thought. And yet this Platonic nightmare, I hold, possesses an alarming contemporary relevance. For the general public is being reduced to a state where people not only are unable to find out about the truth but also become unable even to *search* for the truth because they are satisfied with deception and trickery that have determined their convictions, satisfied with a fictitious reality created by design through the abuse of language. This, says Plato, is the worst thing that the sophists are capable of wreaking upon mankind by their corruption of the word.

There is now the ancient saying *corruptio optimi pessima,* "the best, corrupted, becomes the worst". Those who have some notion about the worst must also, according to this saying, have a notion about what is best. We have to say, of course, that Plato is not simply taking an anti-sophist stance. More decisive is the intensity of his prior positive affirmation; his unwavering strong *opposition* can fully be comprehended only in view of his own *position* regarding the overriding importance of the *good* that is endangered and threatened by the sophists.

With this, indeed, we touch on his most basic convictions, convictions relative to the value and meaning of human existence as such. This we cannot discuss here at any length. Still, I wish to sum up Plato's stance in three brief statements:

*The First Statement:* To perceive, as much as possible, all things as they really are and to live and act according to this truth (truth, indeed, not as something abstract and "floating in thin air" but as the unveiling of reality) — in this consists the good of man; in this consists a meaningful human existence.

*The Second Statement:* All men are nurtured, first and foremost, by the truth, not only those who search for knowledge—the scientists and the philosophers. Everybody who yearns to live as a true *human being* depends on this nourishment. Even society as such is sustained by the truth publicly proclaimed and upheld.

*The Third Statement:* The natural *habitat* of truth is found in interpersonal communication. Truth lives in dialogue, in discussion, in conversation—it resides, therefore, in language, in the word. Consequently, the well-ordered human existence, including especially its social dimension, is essentially based on the well-ordered language employed. A well-ordered language here does not primarily mean its formal perfection, even though I tend to agree with Karl Kraus when he says that every correctly placed comma is decisive. No, a language is well ordered when its words express reality with as little distortion and as little omission as possible.

These three statements may also be considered the foundation of that community of teachers and students established by Plato in the grove of Akademos, the foundation, that is, of the Platonic Academy. But as soon as I use the term *academy,* I do not speak about Plato alone. The term implies an original model from which everything "academic" in the world, up to the present day, derives its name, whether properly so or not. Of course, our contemporary universities, our institutions of higher learning, differ substantially from the original academy of ancient Greece. Still, the term *academic* expresses something that remained unchanged throughout the centuries, something that can be identified quite accurately. It means that in the midst of society there is expressly reserved an area of truth, a sheltered space for the autonomous study of reality, where it is possible, without restrictions, to examine, investigate, discuss, and express what is true about any thing — a space, then, explicitly protected against all potential special interests and invading influences, where hidden agendas have no place, be they collective or private, political, economic, or ideological. At this time in history we have been made aware amply, and forcefully as well, what consequences ensue when a society does or does not provide such a "refuge". Clearly, this is indeed a matter of freedom — not the whole of freedom, to be sure, yet an essential and indispensable dimension of freedom. Limitations and restrictions imposed from the outside are intolerable enough; it is even more depressing for the human spirit when it is made impossible to express and share, that is, to declare publicly, what according to one's best knowledge and clear conscience is the truth about things. All this hardly needs any specific explanation at all.

Such a space of freedom needs not only a guarantee from the outside, from the political power that thus imposes limits on itself. Such a space of freedom also depends on the requirement that freedom be constituted—and defended—within its own domain. By "defended" we mean here not against any threat from the outside but against dangers arising—disturbingly!—within the scholarly domain itself, dangers we have discussed above.

In this precisely consists the irreplaceable achievement of all institutions of higher learning in view of the *bonum commune,* the common good!

"Academic" must mean "antisophistic" if it is to mean anything at all. This implies also opposition to anything that could destroy or distort the nature of the word as communication and its unbiased openness to reality. In this respect we are well able to pronounce the general principle and at the same time to be very specific: opposition is required, for instance, against every partisan simplification, every ideological agitation, every blind emotionality; against seduction through well-turned yet empty slogans, against autocratic terminology with no room for dialogue, against personal insult as an element of style (all the more despicable the more sophisticated it is), against the language of evasive appeasement and false assurance (which Karl Jaspers considered a form of modern sophistry), and not least against the jargon of the revolution, against categorical conformism, and categorical nonconformism: Do we have to go on?

Clearly, none of these challenges can easily be translated into the organized approach of practical action. As the threat is elusive — Plato's experience throughout his life! — so also are the means to resist it. And yet, all this is of eminent political importance. At stake here is the purpose of our institutions of higher learning. Indeed, they are entities not to themselves within the framework of society but to help determine society's overall condition. Their task, then, is to live out a paradigmatic model of conditions that sustain and nourish the structure of the political commonwealth at large: namely, the free interpersonal communication anchored in the truth of reality — the reality of the world around us, the reality of ourselves, and the reality of God as well.

# KNOWLEDGE AND FREEDOM

T HE EXPRESSION *science and freedom,* as used here and now, has a certain opposition in mind. It aims at an opponent who not only denies the freedom of science in theory but also threatens, limits, and destroys this freedom in practice.

In order to discuss this antagonistic situation with rational arguments and not simply to offer a "demonstration" (the ambiguity of this term, *demonstration,* intimately relates to our topic!), we have to comprehend clearly the opposing position, not only in its actual appearance but also in its roots. Only then will it become clear of what kind and what substance the *one* counterargument has to be, an argument that alone would be adequate to address and disprove the innermost conviction of the opponent.

This is not meant to sound simply like a general or "purely academic" reflection, the way it may appear at first. The critical literature on the totalitarian workers' state, right from the beginning, has said it again and again: that it is not at all some suddenly appearing oddity but rather that it fundamentally expresses openly what traditional society itself holds as "a secret and hidden view", for example, the overriding and absolute concern

with economic issues; that the East has given form
and reality to what the West in truth is thinking;
that we, "in our justified struggle against the Soviet slave state, are handicapped by *one* thing",
namely, by the very same tendencies in our own
society. These are three ideas chosen at random—
from a historico-critical volume on the Soviet
workers' state, from a prisoner's report, and from
a polemical pamphlet on freedom. No doubt, we
are dealing here with rather overwrought formu-
lations. Still, they bring home the fact that any rational discussion of the Soviet regime will have to
consider a somewhat complicated situation.

It might happen, for example, that unexpectedly you feel forced, if you want to disprove your
opponent, to revise your own premises. An experience of this kind, I think, is indeed waiting for
those who set out to analyze the enslavement of
science by the totalitarian workers' states. To be
more specific: those who try to argue against this
enslavement, through which the freedom of science is compromised, will have to face some arguments that can be overcome only by correcting
certain notions commonly and for a long time,
even for centuries, accepted by Western civiliza-
tion. When we say, "argue", we do not mean political struggle or active or passive resistance but
*rational discussion* only. Those notions to be cor-

rected contradict certain views up to now unchallenged in the Western world; they are in conflict, that is, with the thoughts not only of the great teachers of Christianity, Augustine no less than Thomas Aquinas, but also of Plato and Aristotle. Those ancient and these modern views both quite specifically speak to our topic here, namely, the nature of knowledge as such, and the relationship between knowledge and freedom.

My thesis here, in positive terms, is this: the decay of the freedom of science as it occurs in the totalitarian workers' states can be adequately counteracted, in the area of rational argumentation, only through the restoration of certain fundamental insights that have their origin in the premodern tradition of Western culture.

These insights shall be discussed here, though perforce in summary terms only. One of them, the most important, is found in Aristotle's *Metaphysics*. The first page of this book—we may be justified to see in it one of the "canonical" texts of the Western mind—already mention the freedom of knowledge. But let us be more precise. What is discussed there is a *specific* knowledge, a specific search for cognition and a specific attempt to gain knowledge: the one that among all the others is supremely free; the one, even, that alone can be called free, and "obviously" so. This would be a knowledge that has as its object the whole of reality, the fundamental reasons of all that is. A knowledge driven by the question as to the essence and the being of all that exists, absolutely and ultimately. A knowledge attempted when the innermost core of the human spirit directs all power of cognition toward the totality of all things, toward the roots and reasons of reality as such; which means: when the power of cognition reaches out to its most adequate and complete and unlimited object. We are talking here about "knowledge pure and absolute", not confined to any individual object, and yet in its dynamism embracing all individual acts of cognition that reach out to some specific and concrete object or aspect of reality, including not least the so-called scientific knowledge. In short, we are talking here about that kind of knowledge called by Aristotle the "most authentically *philosophic*". It should also appear that we are not talking about something isolated and "metaphysical" (Aristotle himself, as is well known, neither knows nor uses this term at all). We are dealing here with the intrinsic "power of cognition" as such, the power moving *within* all concrete experiences and insights and giving them consistency and unity, as it is oriented toward its proper object, the "totality of all that is" (*Gegenstand im Ganzen*).

It is this kind of knowledge that Aristotle declares "alone truly free". The question arises: What does "free" mean here? We have reached, indeed, the critical and decisive point of our problem. "Free", says Aristotle—expressing, we think, a very ancient view, for instance, formulated also by his teacher, Plato, and later dominating the entire Western way of thinking—means the same here as "nonpractical". Praxis means the achievement of purposes; whatever *serves* its purpose is practical. That kind of knowledge, however, that is oriented toward the fundamental reasons of the world, and such knowledge alone, does *not* "serve" any purpose (so he affirms). It would even be impossible and unthinkable to employ it for any practical use at all, "For its reason to be lies entirely in itself." To exist, not in dependence on anything "without" but by and for reasons entirely "within"—this is precisely what human language calls "freedom".

This incredibly concise paragraph of Aristotle's *Metaphysics* (just twenty-some lines) lists, however, some further characteristics of that free and nonpractical knowledge, not to be omitted here. Aristotle adds this: knowledge that envisions the totality of all there is, proceeding by and for its own inherent reasons and thus truly free—such knowledge can never be achieved completely and perfectly by any human being; it is never fully at the disposal of man; it is, therefore, not something entirely within the human sphere, since human existence itself is subject and beholden to many and various needs and wants. One would have to say, according to Aristotle, that God alone could possess such knowledge in a perfect degree, it being oriented toward the divine root in all things anyway. This is the very reason why no other science could claim the same eminence and dignity as the philosophical endeavor, although all of them are of greater necessity: *necessariores omnes, dignior nulla* (as the Latin of the *versio antiqua* has it). So says Aristotle.

In this we see the outlines of a worldview in which the notion "freedom of science" finds its origin. "Origin", however, does not mean here only the historical source—though this, too, must not be overlooked.

The second chapter of Aristotle's *Metaphysics* has in fact, and for the first time in Western thought, outlined a connection between the two concepts of "freedom" and "science". Thomas Aquinas, fifteen hundred years later, commenting on this same chapter, formulated the definition of the *artes liberales* (from which term, of course, derived the medieval name of the academic philosophical faculty, "Faculty of the Arts"). And when John Henry Newman, one hundred years ago, in his book *The Idea of a University*—by now a classic—spoke of "liberal knowledge or a gentleman's knowledge", he explicitly placed himself within this same tradition.

Of more importance, however, than tracing the historical origin of the notion—or rather the claim—of the freedom of science seems to me the truth that it would necessarily lose its legitimacy and inherent credibility as soon as it was severed from its origin, namely, from the foundation of that total worldview. Just such a separation, I hold, occurred at the inception of the modern era.

This fundamental worldview we are discussing here may even more appropriately be seen as a conception regarding the *essence of man* and the meaning of human existence. In an attempt to summarize this worldview in a few brief sentences, we might state the following:

*First:* Even though man is on the whole a practice-oriented being—dependent on the ability to make the things of this world serve his vital needs, nevertheless, his true enrichment does not derive from the technical exploitation of nature's wealth but rather from the purely theoretical cognition of reality. Man's existence becomes more fulfilled the more he can explore and understand reality. He actualizes his essence in the purest form whenever he acts as a "knowing" being, so much so that even his final perfection and fulfillment will consist of an act of cognition: life eternal is called a "contemplation", a *visio*. This is not at all a specifically Christian and theological notion; it can also be found in Aristotle. Anaxagoras states this in his own manner when to the question, "To what purpose are you in this world?" he answers, "To behold the sun, the moon, and the sky"— presumably speaking not about astronomy but rather about the order of the world as a whole.

*Second:* Whenever man engages in the pursuit of theoretical cognition, he most eminently does what he himself, most intimately and authentically, wishes and desires (in which, really, consists the notion of "freedom": to do what you yourself want to do!). Consequently, not only would we consider all true knowledge "free"—the more so the more it is theoretical knowledge—but also *man himself* is all the more free, the more he engages in the pursuit of theoretical knowledge, aimed at the truth and nothing else. Common experience confirms this: whenever someone contemplates reality in pure pursuit of knowledge and without regard for immediate practical purposes; whenever someone, oblivious of possible usefulness, disadvantages, danger, or even death, is able to say, "So it is; this is the truth" (e.g., "The Emperor has no clothes!'")—then we witness, in an eminent degree, human freedom in action. To set us free: this power, according to a venerable pronouncement, is inherent in the truth.

This has been formulated continuously and ever anew in the history of Western thought. Martin Heidegger, too, speaks within the context of this tradition when he sees the very essence of truth anchored in freedom.

*Third:* There exist degrees of cognition—and so also degrees of freedom gained in cognition. The highest degree would be realized should our cognitive faculties completely grasp their proper and perfect object. At the same time there would be attained the highest degree of freedom: man would do in a most perfect way what he essentially desires to do. We are speaking in a conditional mode. For this ultimate goal can *never* be reached during man's corporeal and historical existence, even though it sustains the dynamic drive of this same existence throughout. This is the meaning of Aristotle's statement: that the quest aimed at the foundation of reality as such is a "question always open and raised anew, throughout the past, in the present, and for all time to come". To which Thomas Aquinas in the Middle Ages added this profound commentary: precisely because the answer can never be within our complete disposition, we pursue such wisdom for its own sake. (This implies also, regarding the final and definitive answers given by the exact sciences, that we do not really and fully explore these answers "for their own sakes", as if they would contain their meaning entirely and perfectly in themselves.)

At this juncture, I believe, something very decisive has been stated about *science* (in the strict sense of the word). The exactness of its answers notwithstanding, it does not represent the highest form of knowledge. With regard to freedom as well, it occupies some middle ground, assuming almost a certain ambiguous position. We see this in two respects:

*One*: Should man limit himself to scientific knowledge in the strictest sense, he may incur the danger of losing his openness for the really unlimited object of his cognitive faculties. In other words, there exists a specific form of mental bondage springing from an exclusive ideal of "strict science".

*Two*: It does not infringe upon the nature of science to be employed for purposes other than its own pure reasons. No injustice is done when science accepts tasks belonging in the field of practicalities, be it the field of politics, of economics, of technology, or of the military. Science does not come to an end with this, while philosophy—

being concerned with reality as such, with the essential object of all cognition, pursued for its own sake—yes, philosophy would be destroyed *eo ipso* by such servitude. It may seem at times that it is made to serve, but what is thus pressed into service is no longer philosophy. In science, too, in its innermost core, there is in the same way an element that cannot be taken into service; this is the philosophical element of all *theoria,* directed toward truth and nothing else. This means that science, by its nature, has a claim on freedom on account of its being theoretical, not practical.

This now is the quintessence of our reflection so far: the freedom of knowledge is intimately connected, is even identical, with the latter's theoretical character. Those who infringe upon or destroy the freedom of science can do so only by infringing upon or destroying the theoretical character of science. But the reverse also holds true: those who renounce the theoretical character of their quest for knowledge or declare it of no consequence in view of practical considerations really abandon all possibility of justifying the claim that science must be free.

We find ourselves in this rather strange situation in consequence of certain theses proclaimed at the beginning of the "modern era" and since then made an integral part of modern thinking. Admittedly, such theses did not appear without some legitimate reasons; nevertheless, we may still consider them false or at least in need of correction. More specifically, I am thinking of the statement in Descartes' *Discours de la Méthode:* the place of the old theoretical philosophy should be taken by a new and "practical" approach, so that we may be empowered to become the masters and proprietors of nature *(par laquelle . . . nous pourrions . . . nous rendre comme maîtres et possesseurs de la nature).* This thought reappears almost verbatim in the thesis of American pragmatism that all human knowledge, within the framework of the "intellectual enterprise", should be seen as an instrument only; that the purpose of all intellectual efforts should be "to safeguard our life and the enjoyment of life"; and, above all, that philosophy basically purports not to gain knowledge of the world but to find ways to dominate it. Let me quote a third thesis: "Any scientist who concerns himself with abstract problems must never forget that the purpose of all science consists of satisfying the needs of society." Probably, nobody will contend that there is any essential difference between Descartes' and Dewey's theses and the latter quote—culled, not without some mischievous intent, from the *Great Soviet Encyclopedia.*

All these statements obviously deny the theoretical character of knowledge. (Incidentally, if you approach reality with only the intention to become "master and proprietor", you are entirely unable to look at the totality of the world and the essence of all things in a purely theoretical manner, interested in truth alone and nothing else.) But freedom as well has become impossible; more precisely, it has become impossible to defend this freedom with convincing arguments.

Science in the totalitarian workers' states finds itself constantly pressed to answer the inquisitional question as to what it contributes to the five-year plan. This is nothing else but the strictest consequence of Descartes' statement about the philosophy of the *maître et possesseur de la nature.*

The specter of a certain extreme possibility is arising here, a possibility, it seems, no longer entirely foreign to our experience. It is the knowledge of truth, indeed, that sets the human mind free—and once this conviction is lost or forgotten, then it may happen that the very notion of "freedom" appears to our thinking dubious and vague, even incomprehensible: I do not know any more what it means. Thus we read with dismay in the final notes of André Gide the entry: "There are thousands who are willing to sacrifice their lives to bring about better conditions for this world—more justice, a fairer distribution of temporal goods, and, I hesitate to add, more freedom, *because I do not clearly know what this means.*" Yet the question how to interpret this enigmatic remark will remain unanswered here.

My sole aim was to show that the notion "freedom of science" springs, perhaps unexpectedly, from very deep roots indeed, and that the radical challenge we have to face nowadays demands a defense aware of these roots.

There is a memorable statement, spelling out in touching terms these roots, roots that constitute the ultimate freedom of the knowing mind. The statement is memorable above all because of the man who uttered or rather wrote it, and also because of its exceptional circumstances. The man in question is an eminent representative of Western thought and culture; he was of Roman stock, received his education in Athens, and then, at the court of a German prince, tried to hand on the wisdom of antiquity to the upcoming era: Boethius. And the circumstances? A prison cell. The incarcerated Boethius, awaiting his execution, assures himself of his ultimate indestructible freedom, stating, "The human soul, in essence, enjoys its highest freedom when it remains in the contemplation of God's mind."